Caught Reading

Worktext 3

Mir Tamim Ansary

Upper Saddle River, New Jersey
www.globefearon.com

Project Editor: Brian Hawkes
Editorial Assistants: Jennifer Keezer, Jenna Thorsland
Art Supervision: Sharon Ferguson
Production Editor: Regina McAloney
Electronic Page Production: José López
Manufacturing Supervisor: Mark Cirillo
Cover Design: Sharon Ferguson
Illustrator: Fred Willingham

Copyright © 2000 by Globe Fearon, Inc., One Lake Street, Upper Saddle River, New Jersey, 07458, www.globefearon.com. All rights reserved. No part of this book may be reproduced or transmitted in any form or by any means, electronic or mechanical, including photocopying, recording, or by any information storage and retrieval system, without permission in writing from the publisher. Printed in the United States of America.   4 5 6 7 8 9 10 04 03 02 01
ISBN 0-130-23275-0

CONTENTS

	INTRODUCTION	4
1.	At a Bus Stop One Day	6
2.	The Thing in the Box	10
3.	What's a Little Sister For?	12
4.	A New Drink	17
5.	More Words to Know	20
6.	A Problem for Tom	21
7.	What the Kids Saw	26
8.	Graffiti Guy	29
9.	Luis Tells a Fish Story	33
10.	At the Big Mouth Truck Stop	35
11.	Saturday Night	40
12.	Luis Gets a Job	43
13.	Luis and the Big Bike Sale	48
14.	The Baseball Player, 1	51
15.	The Baseball Player, 2	56
16.	A Card for Carmen	58
17.	Inez Meets a Boy	63
	Memory Chips	66

INTRODUCTION

421!—That's how many words you have learned since you started **Caught Reading**, and you have read more than 30 stories. Now, learn more words so you can read more stories. Go right on into **Caught Reading the third time.**

So far, your teacher or reading helper has read you the directions before and after each story. Now you will slowly take over this job. By **Chapter 6** of this book, you will be reading all the directions yourself. Your teacher or a reading helper will still help you learn the **Words to Know** before each story. But you will be able to read everything else.

Words to Know

Today, you will learn some of the words you need for reading the directions. These are words you have already seen and heard. You have seen and heard them in **Caught Reading the first time** and **Caught Reading the second time.** If you have been following along as your teacher or a reading helper read directions, you may already be reading these words.

	Look	Say	Picture	Write
attack at-tack	☐	☐	☐	_____
below be-low	☐	☐	☐	_____
circle cir-cle	☐	☐	☐	_____
group	☐	☐	☐	_____
introduction in-tro-duc-tion	☐	☐	☐	_____
letter let-ter	☐	☐	☐	_____
read	☐	☐	☐	_____
same	☐	☐	☐	_____
sentence sen-tence	☐	☐	☐	_____

	Look	Say	Picture	Write
sound	☐	☐	☐	_____
story sto-ry	☐	☐	☐	_____
these	☐	☐	☐	_____
together to-geth-er	☐	☐	☐	_____
word	☐	☐	☐	_____
write	☐	☐	☐	_____

Word Attack

+s   Write **s** after the words below.

letter _____   group _____

sentence _____   sound _____

word _____   read _____

+ing   Now write **ing** after **read**. _____

+er, +ing   Add the endings **er** and **ing** to **write**. But first you have to take away the **e** from **write**. Write the words below.

write + er _____   write + ing _____

2=1   Put together the words below to make new words. Write them below.

a + like = _____   a + part = _____

a + long = _____

McR

Tear out the **McR** chips for the new words you have learned. They are on **page 67** and are marked **IA**. (**I** stands for **Introduction**.) Tear out a new group of chips every time you learn a new group of words. When you see **McR**, you know it is time to program your memory to hold more words.

1. AT A BUS STOP ONE DAY

Word Attack

Try This

Some words end with one vowel, another letter, and then **e**. Here is something that works with many (but not all) words like this. The first vowel sounds like its own name. The **e** at the end makes no sound. Look for this in the words below. Circle the vowels that sound like their own names. Put **X** over the vowels you cannot hear.

        made   time   vote   use   these

Try it with a new word. Read: **here.** Write it _____

it   You know the word **it**. One of the new **Words to Know** is just **s + it**. Try reading this word: **sit**. Now write the words below on the lines. Circle the letter group that is the same in the two words.

sit _____ hit _____

game   You know how the word **game** sounds. It sounds the same in one of the new words. Try reading this word: **name**. Now write the words below and circle the letter group that you find in all the words.

name _____ game _____

same _____

night   You know how the letter group **ight** sounds in the word **night**. Now read this new word: **right**. Write the words below. Circle the letter group that you find in all the words.

right _____ night _____

light _____

old   You know the word **sold**. Take away **s** and you have the word **old.**   Write this new word in the sentence.

My grandma is _____ .

Words to Know

	Look	Say	Picture	Write
as	☐	☐	☐	_____
box	☐	☐	☐	_____
down	☐	☐	☐	_____
has	☐	☐	☐	_____
here	☐	☐	☐	_____
leave	☐	☐	☐	_____
name	☐	☐	☐	_____
old	☐	☐	☐	_____
open	☐	☐	☐	_____
o-pen				
or	☐	☐	☐	_____
right	☐	☐	☐	_____
sit	☐	☐	☐	_____
thing	☐	☐	☐	_____

Word Attack

+ s Write **s** after the words below. Write the new words.

leave _____   open _____

sit _____   thing _____

+es After most words that end in **x**, write **es**, not just **s.** Try it now. Write **box** with an **es** ending.

box + es = _____

2=1 Put these words together. Write the new words.

no+thing = _____

some+thing = _____

some + one = _____

+ 's If Tom has something, you say it is **Tom's**. To make this word, you write the ending **'s** after **Tom.** Write the new word in the sentence below.

This is _____ car.

7

1. AT A BUS STOP ONE DAY

Tom is at a bus stop one day. A man with some boxes comes up. He puts his things next to Tom. He sits down.

Time goes by. Then more time goes by. "Where is that bus?" Tom asks. He finds it hard to just sit and wait. He gets up to look for the bus. The other man gets up, too. But he is giving up on the bus. He walks away. He leaves a big box next to Tom.

Tom calls after the man. "Wait!" he says. "You there! Did you forget this thing? Don't you want it?"

The man keeps walking. What **is** it about this guy? Is he **trying** to get away from the box? Should Tom be scared? Then he thinks, No, *the man is just old. Maybe he can't hear me.*

So Tom gets up and runs after the man. But as he runs, he sees his bus coming. He can't get to the man and back to the bus. Tom really needs to get on that bus. So back he goes.

He runs as fast as he can. But he doesn't make it! The bus leaves without him.

Tom has the box. But he doesn't know what to do with it. There is no name on it. He knows nothing about the man. If he opens the box, he can see what is in it. Maybe he will find out something about the man. But he doesn't think it is right to open a box that is not his.

Tom sits down to wait for the next bus. He thinks and thinks about the box. He thinks about the old man, too. He looked like a man with money. Tom looks at the box. What is in it? What should Tom do with it? When the next bus comes, Tom will have to get on. Should he leave the box here or what? The old man may come back for it. He will look for it where he put it. But then Tom thinks, *Lots of people go by this bus stop. Someone will get the box. But who says it will be the old man?*

Just then Tom's bus comes. So Tom gets on the bus. He takes the box along. Already he thinks of it as his box. He does not know what is in it. But he is going to find out. Then it will be his.

You Make the Call

Get together with a group of friends who have read the story. Talk about the problem that Tom has. What should he do with the box? Should he take it home, or should he leave it at the bus stop? What would you do if you were Tom? Why?

Think About It

These sentences are about the story. Write them below in the order that they come up in the story. Read the story one more time if you need to.

The bus leaves without Tom.

A man with some boxes comes up.

Tom runs after the man.

Tom gets on the bus with the box.

The man gives up and walks away.

_____

_____

_____

_____

_____

_____

Remembering Details

Write words from the story on the lines. Look back at the story if you have to.

Tom is at a _____ stop in this story.

A man leaves a _____ next to Tom.

The box has no _____ on the outside.

Maybe the man can't hear Tom because the

man is _____ .

9

2. THE THING IN THE BOX

Tom walks into his house with his box. His family has already started dinner. "Sit down," says his grandma. "What do you have in the box?"

Tom tells the story of the man at the bus stop. He tells his grandma how the man did not wait for the bus. Tom tells her how the man walked away and did not take the box with him.

"Open it," says his sister. "I want to see what's in there."

"What if it's something bad?" Tom says with a laugh.

"Good or bad, you can't keep it," says his dad. "We have to give it back to the man."

Tom says, "Forget it, Dad. We don't know where to find the man. We can't give it back to him."

Tom's sister says, "What if there is money in the box?"

"I want it to be a CD player," says Tom.

"No, you don't," says his sister. "If you have money, you can get a CD player."

"If you have a CD player, you can get money," Tom says. "You can always sell a CD player."

"What?" Tom's sister gets mad. "You're going to sell our CD player?"

"It's my CD player," says Tom. "I can do what I want with it."

"CD player?" Grandma asks.

Tom's dad laughs. "Kids, kids! You don't know what's in that box. But I guess it's OK to open it. We will see what is in it. Then we will talk about what to do with it."

Tom opens the box. Then he backs away—fast!

Tom's sister looks into the box. She says. "OK, Tom. I give up. You can keep this."

Grandma looks into the box. "My word!" she says. "There is nothing in this box but a really old fish!"

"You call that a fish?" says Tom.

"What do you call it?" his grandma asks.

Tom takes another careful look into the box.

"I call it—**The Thing Without a Name**," he says.

What Do You Think?

Meet with a friend or in a small group. Talk about what you think Tom should do with the box. Do you think it was right for Tom to open the box? Give your reasons why.

Putting Ideas in Order

Here are four sentences from the story. Write them in the order that they come up in the story.

"I call it—**The Thing Without a Name**," he says.

"It's my CD player," says Tom.

Tom's sister looks into the box.

Tom opens the box.

_____

_____

_____

_____

_____

_____

Find the One Big Idea

One of the sentences below best says what the story is about. It gives the big idea of the story. Find that sentence, and write it below.

Tom finds something he has wanted for a long time.

Tom and his sister do not get along.

The thing in the box is a thing no one wants.

_____

_____

_____

3. WHAT'S A LITTLE SISTER FOR?

Word Attack

get   One of your new **Words to Know** ends the same way as the word **get**. See if you can read this word: **let**. Now write the new word in the sentence below.

_____ me go.

fast   You know the word **fast**. Try to read this word: **last**.

Now write the two words below, and circle the letter group you see in both words.

fast _____   last _____

letter   You have seen the letter group **etter** in **letter**. It sounds the same in **better**. Read **better**. Write the two words below, and circle the letter group **etter**.

letter _____   better _____

NEW   **made**   Remember what works with many words that end with a vowel: another letter and then **e**. The first vowel has a **long** sound. The **e** at the end has no sound. Use this to attack one of the new words. Try to read **made**. Now write the new word in the sentence.

Jared _____ a good dinner.

Take a Guess

There are times when you can tell what a new word is by reading it in a sentence. The other words in the sentence can help you guess the word. Read the sentence below. Try to guess the word in dark letters. The word **cook** can help you. Think about where a cook may be.

The cook is in the **kitchen**.

What would you guess the new word to be? Maybe your guess is **kitchen**. How do you find out if you are right? Do these things:

   1. Say the word you guess. Think of the sound it starts with: **k**.

2. Look at the sound that starts the word in the sentence. Is it the same? Yes. The word **kitchen** starts with **k.** So far, **kitchen** looks like the right word.
3. Now look at the other letters in the word. Look for sounds and letter groups that you know. Do you see an ending you have seen before?

The word is **kitchen**. Write it. _____

Words to Know

	Look	Say	Picture	Write
better bet-ter	☐	☐	☐	_____
Carmen Car-men	☐	☐	☐	_____
every ev-er-y	☐	☐	☐	_____
had	☐	☐	☐	_____
Inez I-nez	☐	☐	☐	_____
kitchen kitch-en	☐	☐	☐	_____
last	☐	☐	☐	_____
let	☐	☐	☐	_____
made	☐	☐	☐	_____
show	☐	☐	☐	_____
so	☐	☐	☐	_____
too	☐	☐	☐	_____

Word Attack

2=1 You know the words **any, every, thing**, and **where**. From these words, you can make three new words. Write the new words on the lines below.

any + thing = _____

every + thing = _____

every + where = _____

+'s Write **'s** after **Inez** to make **Inez's**. Write the new word in the sentence.

You can walk to _____ house from here.

+ s Write **s** after these words to make two new words.

let _____

sister _____

ed Write **call** with an **ed** ending: _____

2=1 You can write **is not** as one word: **isn't**. Write an **X** over the letter you leave out of **is not** to write **isn't**.

This _____ my house.

_____ it your house?

McR

Tear out the memory chips for Chapter 3. Practice with the **A** side first. Ask for help if you need it. Then try to read the words on the **B** side. Review your memory chips from the Introduction and Chapter 1 as well.

3. WHAT'S A LITTLE SISTER FOR?

Carmen is looking at TV. Her sister Inez comes in. Inez is 14—friendly and happy, most of the time. She sits down next to Carmen. "What is this show?" Inez asks.

"It's called **The Thing Without a Name**," says Carmen.

Inez gives her sister a long, dark look. "You don't really like this sorry show, do you? I don't. The people are so out of it. There is a better show on at this time. It's a game show. Have you ever seen **Anything for a Laugh**? It's so good! There is a boy on the show who is so good-looking! There is another one—he's good-looking, too. You just have to see him. Don't you want to see them, Carmen?"

"No," says Carmen. The idea of Inez's show leaves her cold.

But Inez keeps talking about it. At last, Carmen gets up. She lets Inez have the TV. "I will start dinner," she says.

Carmen goes into the kitchen and starts to cook.

But Inez comes right after her. "What are you cooking?" she asks. "Can I help? I know another thing we can make. It's better. Let me show you. I made it just the other day."

And she comes closer.

"Inez," says Carmen, "I have had it up to here with you. Every time I look, there you are. Everywhere I go, you come after me. Everything I do, you want to try it, too. How come you will not let me be?"

"Because," says Inez, "I'm your little sister. This is what little sisters do, isn't it? I am just doing my job!"

What Do You Think

Meet with a friend or in a small group. Talk about Inez and Carmen. How are they different? Are there ways they are alike? Which one are you most like, and why?

Remembering Details

Write words from the story on each line. Look back at the story if you have to.

Carmen is looking at a show called _____.

Inez wants to see a show called _____.

Carmen gives up on her show and goes into the _____ to cook.

Describe It

To **describe** something is to give details about it. Words that describe help you picture what you are reading. Take this sentence:

Inez is 14—friendly and happy, most of the time.

Friendly and **happy** are words that describe Inez. They help you picture what Inez is like. Find two words that describe the look that Inez gives her sister. Write them on the line below.

_____

_____

Inez talks about two shows on TV. Here some words she uses. Write the words next to the things they describe.

    sorry   so good   good-looking   out of it

The Thing Without a Name: _____

The people on Carmen's show: _____

Anything for a Laugh: _____

A boy on **Anything for a Laugh**: _____

4. A NEW DRINK

"OK," says Carmen. "Show me what you want to cook."

"It's a—it's a—" Inez stops to think. "It's a drink," she says. "A new drink."

"Is this a hot drink?" Carmen asks. "I don't know if you should be cooking over a hot—"

"It's not hot," says Inez. "It's a cold drink."

"Is that so?" says Carmen. "What is in this drink?"

"I can't tell you about it," says Inez. "You just have to see. Let me make some." Inez starts to work on the drink. "You put in a little of this—" she says. "You put in a little of that—" She is working faster. "And a little of this—" she goes on. "And some of this—and a lot of that—"

Carmen smiles. "Inez, these things don't go together. You are making this up as you go."

"No, I'm not. I made some the other day. It's good. Believe me." She puts in one more thing and says, "There! Have some of this, Carmen."

"Not me," says Carmen. "You have some."

Inez looks at the drink for a long time. But she does not drink it. She says, "It has to sit here a little. Then it gets really good."

"I am going back to the TV," says Carmen.

"Me, too," says Inez.

After the TV show, the sisters go back to the kitchen. They see the family dog. It is just drinking the last of Inez's drink.

"No!" Inez lets out a cry. She goes for the dog. But Carmen stops her.

"It's OK, Inez. I don't think you really wanted to drink any of that. I know I didn't. But look how happy you have made the dog."

"See?" says Inez. "What did I tell you? **The Drink Without a Name** is good."

Describe It

Here is an ad for the drink Inez has made up. It needs three more words. Find three words in the story that describe **The Drink Without a Name**. Write the words on the lines.

TRY ... THE DRINK WITHOUT A NAME!

It's _____!   It's _____!   It's _____!

People will like it! Even your dog will like it.

18

Putting Ideas in Order

Here are three things that go on in the story. Write them on the lines in the right order.

Carmen goes back to the TV.

The dog has a drink.

Inez looks at the drink but does not drink it.

Inez says she will make a new drink.

_____
_____
_____
_____
_____
_____

Find the One Big Idea

One of these sentences tells what the story is all about. Find that sentence and write it below.

Inez makes up a drink that is good—but only for dogs.

Inez shows Carmen how to make something new.

Carmen goes back to her TV show.

_____
_____
_____
_____

5. MORE WORDS TO KNOW

After you learn these words, you will be able to read all the directions in this book—both before and after the stories.

	Look	Say	Picture	Write
again a-gain	☐	☐	☐	_____
all	☐	☐	☐	_____
answer an-swer	☐	☐	☐	_____
best	☐	☐	☐	_____
describe de-scribe	☐	☐	☐	_____
detail de-tail	☐	☐	☐	_____
end	☐	☐	☐	_____
guess	☐	☐	☐	_____
each	☐	☐	☐	_____
picture pic-ture	☐	☐	☐	_____
order or-der	☐	☐	☐	_____
remember re-mem-ber	☐	☐	☐	_____
vowel vow-el	☐	☐	☐	_____

Word Attack

+ing   Write **ing** after **remember, order,** and **end**.

_____ _____ _____

+s   Write these words with the ending **s** after them.

vowel _____   detail _____

end _____   ending _____

picture _____   answer _____

6. A PROBLEM FOR TOM

Word Attack

race You have seen the word **race**. You will see the ending sound in **race** in one of the new words, too. It sounds the same here. Try reading this word: **face.** Now write the words below. Circle the letter group that is the same in them.

face _____

race _____

find You know how the letter group **ind** sounds in **find**. This letter group is in one of your new **Words to Know,** and it sounds the same as it does in **find**. Say **m** with **ind** and you have this new word. Try reading the word: **mind**. Write the two words you see below. Circle the letter group **ind** in the two words.

mind _____

find _____

tell You know the word **tell**. Change the first letter to **w**, and you have a new word. Read this word: **well**. Write the words below. Circle the letter group you see in all three words.

well _____ tell _____ sell _____

should You can attack the new word **would**. It sounds like **should** and ends with the same letter group. Try reading the word: **would**. Now write the words below on the lines. Circle the letters that are the same in them.

would _____

should _____

21

Take a Guess

Maybe you can guess the word **wrong** by reading it in a sentence. The first letter in this word is one that you can't hear. So don't go by the first letter. Use the other words to help you guess. The words **not right** may help you get it.

This answer is not right. It's **wrong**.

Did you guess the new word? Write it. _____

Words to Know

	Look	Say	Picture	Write
face	☐	☐	☐	_____
from	☐	☐	☐	_____
guy	☐	☐	☐	_____
mind	☐	☐	☐	_____
said	☐	☐	☐	_____
saw	☐	☐	☐	_____
than	☐	☐	☐	_____
well	☐	☐	☐	_____
were	☐	☐	☐	_____
why	☐	☐	☐	_____
would	☐	☐	☐	_____
wrong	☐	☐	☐	_____

Word Attack

2=1 You know the words below. Write them together to make four new words.

any + way = _____

to + day = _____

every + one = _____

some + how = _____

+ s You know the word **believe**. Write **s** after it.

believe + s = _____

's You can write **he is** as one new word: **he's**. You can write **let us** as one new word: **let's**. You can write **that is** as one new word: **that's**. Write the three new words in the sentences below. Then write **X** over the letter in each set of two words that is not in the one word.

he is: Call Tom. I know _____ home.

let us: Everyone, _____ go see Tom.

that is: I think _____ his house.

+es To write **cry** with an **es** ending, change the **y** to **i**. (Do this with most words that end in **y**.) Write the new word.

_____

Now write **try** with an **es** ending.

(Remember: first change **y** to **i**.) _____

23

6. A PROBLEM FOR TOM

Carmen runs into a boy from her class. His name is Tom. "Well, there you are!" she says. "The principal has been looking everywhere for you."

"Why?" asks Tom. "Is something wrong?"

"I should say so!" Carmen goes up to him. "Someone put some graffiti on the wall at school. The principal believes it was you. The principal was not happy when he saw it. He was screaming."

"Me?" cries Tom. Now Tom was not happy. "How can you say a thing like that? I would not write on the school walls. I would not write on any walls—ever! Don't you know me better than that, Carmen?"

"I guess I do," says Carmen. "But the principal doesn't. He asked everyone to come in and see him today. He called the kids in one by one. He had each of us tell him what we know. But one guy did not go in and see him. That one guy was you, Tom. How come you didn't talk to the principal?"

"Because I was not at school today, that's why. I was not feeling well," says Tom. "Anyway, so what if I didn't talk to him. What does that show?"

"He said maybe it shows you have something to hide."

"Man, he's so off-base," says Tom. "I have to talk to him. Somehow, I have to show him that he's wrong about me." Tom's face looks as long as a day without sun.

"Well," says Carmen, "we will think of something on the way. Let's go."

"We?" says Tom. "Are you coming with me?"

"Why not?" says Carmen. "I want to help. Do you mind?"

Tom tries to smile. "Why should I mind? I can use all the help I can get." Tom starts to think. Maybe with some help from Carmen things will be O.K. Together they will find out who did the graffitti.

What Do You Think?

Meet with one or more friends who have read **A Problem for Tom**. Talk about what you would do if you were Carmen. Would you try to help Tom? Why or why not? Carmen says she wants to help Tom. What do you think—can she really help him? Why or why not?

Read It Again

The sentences below ask about the story. Look back at the story to find answers. Use your own words to write the answers on the lines. The first answer is already there.

Why is the graffiti at school a problem for Tom?

<u>The principal thinks he did it.</u>

Why didn't Tom go in and talk to the principal?

_____

Why was Tom not at school today?

_____

How come Carmen is going to go with Tom?

_____

Describe It

A writer may describe one thing by telling how it is like another thing. This can be a good way to tell how people in a story feel. One sentence in **A Problem for Tom** does just this. Here is the sentence.

Tom's face looks as long as a day without sun.

What is this sentence really saying about Tom? Find the answer below. Circle it. Then write it on the line.

Tom does not feel happy.

Tom is a bad boy.

Tom is really sick.

_____

_____

7. WHAT THE KIDS SAW

"I just don't get it," says Tom. "Why does the principal think this graffiti is my work?"

Carmen and Tom are walking to the school.

Carmen says, "For one thing, you did do some graffiti another time. Didn't you?"

"Well—" says Tom. "Yes."

"Didn't they call you **Graffiti Guy**?"

"Well—" says Tom. "Yes. They did. OK? But that was a long time back. I was just a kid. I didn't know any better. I am not the same guy."

"And there is another thing," says Carmen.

"What's that?" Tom stops and looks at her.

"Some kids say they saw you doing it," says Carmen.

"What?" screams Tom. "When? Where? How? What did they say?"

Carmen can see that Tom is getting mad. But she goes on. "They saw some guy last Saturday. That's what they say, anyway. They were going by the school. They looked over, and there he was—writing on the wall. From what I hear, he looked like you."

Tom is walking faster. Now he is getting really hot. "Why would they say a thing like that? Who are these kids? I would like to get a hold of them!"

"And then what?" says Carmen. "What would you do? Hit someone? What good will that do? The principal already thinks of you as **Graffiti Guy**. What will they call you if you start hitting people?"

"I guess it would not look good," Tom says.

"This is not just about looks," says Carmen. "If you hit someone, it will be bad."

"I know." Tom is looking down as he walks. "I just want to know—what's the use? I study hard. I try hard. I am on the baseball team. It's all going to be for nothing. Someone does graffiti. Right away, everyone believes it was me."

"Not everyone," says Carmen. I believe you. That's something, isn't it?"

"I guess."

"Tom, you can't be mad at the kids who said they saw you. They are just telling the principal what they saw. They did see someone. They are not making it up. But they did not see him up close. So you know what I think?"

"What?"

"I think the guy who did this looks like you."

"I see," says Tom. "But how does that help me?"

"It may help you look for him," says Carmen. "In the end, you will have to find the real **Graffiti Guy**. Then people will believe you."

"Yes, but where should I look?" says Tom.

"I don't know," says Carmen. And they keep walking.

What Do You Think?

Carmen does not think Tom did the graffiti. What do you think? Get together with a friend or a group of friends. Talk about it. Look for details in the story that show why you think as you do.

Remembering Details

Words such as **when, where,** and **what** can get you right to the details in a story. In **What the Kids Saw**, the principal hears a story from some kids. The sentences below ask about this story. Read the sentences. Write the answers. Look back at the reading if you have to.

The kids say they saw something. **When** did they see it?
_____

Where were they at the time?
_____

They say they saw a guy. **What** was the guy doing?
_____

What Comes Next?

The sentences below tell four things that **may** come up in the next part of this story. Circle the one thing you think **will** come up in the next part of the story. Read. Write it on the lines. Then talk about it with a friend who has read the story, too. Why do you think as you do? What does your friend think?

Tom will get mad and scream at the principal.

Carmen will get mad and walk away from Tom.

Carmen will find out who really did the graffiti.

The principal will not believe Tom.

_____
_____
_____

8. GRAFFITI GUY

Word Attack

face One of the new **Words to Know** has the same ending sound as **face.** Read, then write the new word, **place,** in the sentence.

I like this _____.

Take a Guess

Read the sentence. Guess the new word from the other words around it.

Where is your sister? **Point** to her.

Write the new word here. _____

Words to Know

	Look	Say	Picture	Write
always al-ways	☐	☐	☐	_____
else	☐	☐	☐	_____
first	☐	☐	☐	_____
Luis Lu-is	☐	☐	☐	_____
move	☐	☐	☐	_____
place	☐	☐	☐	_____
point	☐	☐	☐	_____
self	☐	☐	☐	_____
them	☐	☐	☐	_____
yes	☐	☐	☐	_____

Word Attack

+s Write **s** after each of the words below.

feeling _____   game _____

light _____   place _____

point _____   shop _____

show _____   move _____

1=2 Find two words you know in **someday**. Write them below.

someday = _____ + _____

8. GRAFFITI GUY

Carmen and Tom are walking by some shops. Carmen stops. She points at a shop that sells fish. "Look over there, Tom. What do you see?"

Tom sees a boy writing on the wall.

"He looks a little like me!" says Tom. "Doesn't he?"

"Wait here," says Carmen. She goes over to the boy.

"What are you doing?" she asks.

The boy laughs. "I am writing an ad. What does it look like?"

"An ad for what?" says Carmen.

"An ad for my own self," says the boy. "Who else?"

"On a wall?" says Carmen.

"That's the point!" the boy says. "I want lots of people to see it." He goes right on working. Then he says, "There! That's that. What do you think? Move back a little. That way you can see it better."

Carmen looks up. She sees the ad. The letters are as big as people. She reads the words. They say:

"Luis is the man. Luis is the best. What a hot guy!"

"Are you Luis?" she asks.

"Yes, I am." His face lights up. "I am the man himself. Luis is my name. Writing on walls is my game. I have what it takes and it shows. Who are you?"

"I'm Carmen," she says. "I think I am going to be sick."

"Many people have these feelings at first," Luis tells her. "You will get over it. Already I think you like me. Yes, you do. Don't try to hide it. I know people and I know them well. I'm good that way. I can always tell. So what do you say? Let's go out someday."

Carmen looks Luis over. She says, "How about today?"

"Man! You don't play games, do you? I like that," says Luis. "I have a lot of girls after me, Carmen. But you know what? I will always like you best. Really. Always. Where should we go? I know some good places." When Luis talks, his words come fast, fast, fast.

"I know just the place," says Carmen. "Come on." She calls out, "Tom! Are you coming?"

"Tom?" says Luis. "Who is Tom? And where are we going?"

"You will see," says Carmen. She starts for the school.

What Do You Think?

Carmen is taking Luis in to see the principal. Is she doing the right thing? Meet with one or more friends and talk about it. What would you do if you were Carmen? Why?

Putting Ideas in Order

Here are five sentences from the story. They tell some things that are in the story. But they are not in the right order. Write them on the lines in story order.

"Are you Luis?" she asks.

Carmen looks up and sees the ad.

Tom sees a boy writing on the wall.

"Tom?" says Luis. "Who is Tom?

"I know just the place," says Carmen.

_____

_____

_____

_____

_____

Describe It

Find sentences in the story that describe the things below. Write the sentences on the lines.

What does Luis's ad look like?

_____

How does Luis's face look when he talks to Carmen?

_____

How does Luis sound when he talks?

_____

9. LUIS TELLS A FISH STORY

"Wait," says Luis. "What are we doing here? This is the school! Is this your idea of a good time, Carmen?"

Carmen smiles. "Who said anything about a good time, Luis? I want you to meet someone."

She takes Luis to the principal. Tom comes, too. She says to the principal, "You know the graffiti on the school walls? I think you should talk to these boys. This is Tom. He is the one you wanted to see. This other boy is Luis. He goes to our school, too. I think they look alike, don't you?"

"A little," says the principal. "What's your point?"

"Some people say they saw Tom writing the graffiti. But maybe they saw Luis," says Carmen.

The principal says to Luis, "Well? Let's hear it. What do you know about this graffiti?"

"Graffiti?" says Luis. "Did someone write graffiti on the walls here?"

"Yes," says the principal. "Didn't you see it?"

"No, I didn't see it or hear about it," says Luis. "I was not at school today. Where would I hear about it? I did not do it."

"Why should we believe you?" Carmen asks.

"Because I was home at the time," says Luis. "My sister will back me up. Call her. She saw me come in at 4:00 on Saturday. She saw me leave at 6:00."

"What does that show?" asks Tom.

"It shows that I was home from 4:00 to 6:00. The graffiti was put on that wall at 5:00 on Saturday," says Luis.

The principal makes Luis sit down. "Luis," he says, "you said you didn't even hear about this graffiti. How come you know just when it was put on that wall? You say you know the day and the time. You are telling us a fish story, Luis. The one who did this graffiti is you."

Luis just looks down. He does not look at the principal. He does not look at Carmen or Tom. Luis knows he is telling a fish story. What will he do now?

33

Put Sentences in Order

The sentences below tell four things that take place in the story. Write them in the order that they take place.

Luis says he was at home from 4:00 to 6:00.

The principal asks Luis about the graffiti.

The principal says that Luis did the graffiti.

Carmen takes Luis to the principal.

_____
_____
_____
_____
_____
_____
_____

Find the One Big Idea

What is this story really about? Only one group of words below makes this big point. Find this group of words. Write it on the line.

Luis tries to show that he did not do the graffiti. But what his story really shows is that _____
_____

a. he has a sister.
b. he got home at 4:00 on Saturday.
c. he did the graffiti.

34

McR

10. AT THE BIG MOUTH TRUCK STOP

Word Attack

buy You know how the word **buy** sounds. Try reading the new word: **guy.** Write the word that goes in each sentence below. Circle the letter group that is the same in the words you write.

Tom is a good _____. He will _____ a car.

would You have seen the same letter group in **should** and **would.** Look for it in a new word now. Try reading this word: **could.** Write the three words below on the lines. Circle the letter group that they all have.

could _____ would _____

should _____

wave The word **wave** ends with the letter group **ave**. This letter group does not always sound the way it does in **wave.** But try it in this word: **save.** Is this a word you know? Now write the words below. Circle the letter group that is the same in the two words.

save _____ wave _____

Take a Guess

Can you guess the word in dark letters? Use the other words in the sentences to help you. Think of a word that starts with an **m** sound. It will be something people use when they talk.

Luis talks too much. He has a big **mouth**.

What word did you guess? Write the word. _____

35

Words to Know

	Look	Say	Picture	Write
again a-gain	☐	☐	☐	_____
buy	☐	☐	☐	_____
could	☐	☐	☐	_____
door	☐	☐	☐	_____
food	☐	☐	☐	_____
hand	☐	☐	☐	_____
happen hap-pen	☐	☐	☐	_____
mouth	☐	☐	☐	_____
oh	☐	☐	☐	_____
pull	☐	☐	☐	_____
save	☐	☐	☐	_____

Word Attack

+s Write the words below with **s** at the end.

pull _____ move _____

happen _____

2=1 The words **herself, homework**, and **somewhere** are made up of words you know. Write the two words.

herself _____ _____

homework _____ _____

somewhere _____ _____

+ 's Does **house of Carmen** sound right? Not really. Most of the time, most people would say **Carmen's house**. Write **'s** after **Carmen** to get the new word.

Carmen + ' s = _____

's You can write the two words **she is** as one word: **she's**. Write the one word in the sentence.

This is her house, but _____ not home.

36

10. AT THE BIG MOUTH TRUCK STOP

Carmen and Tom leave the school. Tom is thinking, *I like this girl. I think she likes me.*

He says to Carmen, "Where are you going?"

"I don't know," says Carmen. "Why do you ask?"

"Well, I was thinking we could go somewhere together. It would be just you and I. I know this place we could go. They have good food. We could talk and all. I could get to know you better."

"Why not?" says Carmen. She's thinking, *I don't know what is going to happen but I like this guy.*

Carmen gets into Tom's car and they drive. Tom pulls up at the **Big Mouth Truck Stop.**

"This place has good food?" Carmen can hardly believe what she sees. "This place?" The door of the place looks like a big open mouth.

Tom just stops as he is about to pull the car door open. "You don't like this place? We don't have to go here."

"No, no. It's OK," says Carmen. "I just want to talk. I guess this place is as good as any to talk in."

But she is wrong about that. The **Big Mouth** is not a good place for two people to talk. There is just one big room. In this room are many, many people. All of them are talking and laughing at the same time. Carmen can hardly hear herself think. She and Tom buy some food. Then they sit down face to face.

"So what do you think of this place?" he screams.

"What?" she screams.

He says the words again.

"I like it," she screams. "It's like my house. Lots of sound."

She goes on talking. Tom cannot hear a word she is saying. He just keeps looking at Carmen's face. From time to time, he screams, "Yes, me, too!" He wants to hold her hand. But he doesn't want to move too fast. He is thinking, *I don't want this to end.*

But, at last, Carmen looks up. "Oh!" she says. "Is it 4:00 already? I have to go. I have a lot of homework."

Tom gets up, too. "OK," he says. "But first, let me ask you something."

"Ask away," says Carmen.

"Well," he says, "I have got to hand it to you. You really helped me with the principal. But you hardly know me. Why did you go out of your way to help me?"

Carmen smiles at him. "Let's just say I like a good story," she says. "I really like a happy ending, too."

"If this an ending, I'm not happy," says Tom. "Tell me this is just the start, Carmen."

"All right," said Carmen. "Let's say this is just the start—of something. What happens next?"

"Next?" he says. "Let's go out. How about Saturday?"

"I'll see you at 8:00," she says. At the door, she stops. They go together out the door, hand-in-hand.

Describe It

Read the groups of words below. Only four of them tell something about the **Big Mouth Truck Stop**. Circle these groups. Then write them next to the things they describe.

Tom's car   a big, open mouth

many, many people   a good place to talk

good   laughing and talking

What the door is like _____

What you see in the truck stop _____

What you hear in the truck stop _____

What the food is like _____

What Will Happen Next?

Tom and Carmen say they are going to go out. What do you think will happen when they do? Read the four ideas below. Put a line through two things that you think will **not** happen. Circle two things that you think **may** happen. Write them on the lines. Sit down with some other kids who have read the story. Talk about why you think these things will happen.

The school principal will ask to come along.

Tom and Carmen will have a good time.

Carmen will get mad at Tom.

Tom and Luis will take Carmen out together.

_____
_____
_____
_____
_____

11. SATURDAY NIGHT

Tom shows up at 8:00 on Saturday. This time he has a truck.

"It's my dad's," he says. "My own car is in the shop. You don't mind, do you?"

"Not at all," says Carmen. "Let's go."

After they drive for a time, the truck starts to make a bad sound. Then it stops.

"What is it?" Carmen asks.

"I don't know," says Tom. "Something is wrong with Dad's truck." He looks out. Snow is coming down. "I could walk to a shop," he says. "But I don't want to leave you here in the dark."

"I'll go with you," says Carmen.

"All right. But should we go when it's snowing like this?"

"No," says Carmen. "Let's wait."

They sit without talking. Then Tom says, "I didn't want this to happen, Carmen. I would not try to pull a fast one on you."

"Yes, I know, Tom. I believe you."

"But here we are," he goes on. "Just you and me, you know. We may as well get close. Don't you think?" He takes her hand. His face comes closer and closer.

Carmen pulls away. "I hear something." She sits up.

She looks back. "Tom," she says, "there is someone in the back of your truck."

Tom turns. He makes no sound. He looks through the window. At last, he says, "I think you're right." He opens the door. "I had better take a look."

"Be careful," says Carmen.

The night is cold. It is dark, too. Tom feels a little scared. Carmen looks scared, too. "I have a light somewhere," he says. He finds it and gets it out. He points the light into the back of the truck. He sees something dark and pretty big. He sees it move. Then the dark thing sits up. He can see that it is a little man. No, it is a little woman. No, that is wrong, too. It is a girl.

"Inez!" screams Carmen.

"Who?" says Tom.

"It's my sister, Inez. What are you doing here?"

"I just wanted to come along!" Inez is crying. They help her out of the back. She has snow all over her face. She says, "I just wanted to see where you were going. I didn't know it was going to be so cold back there."

Carmen says, "You had it coming." She is mad.

That night, Carmen and Tom end up at the **Big Mouth Truck Stop**. Inez is with them. It is not what Carmen wanted. It is not what Tom wanted. But Inez is as happy as can be.

"I like your new boyfriend," she tells Carmen when they get home.

What Do You Think?

Put yourself in Tom's or Carmen's place. Picture finding Inez in the back of the truck. How would you feel? Talk about it with a friend or a group of friends. Did anything like this ever happen to you?

Describe It

What is the night like when Carmen and Tom go out? Look for details in the story that describe that night. Write the details below. You can write one word, a group of words, or a sentence. Write three details.

_____

_____

_____

Putting Ideas in Order

The sentences below tell five things that happen in the story. But they are not in the right order. Write them on the lines in the order that they happen in the story.

He points the light into the back of the truck.

The truck starts to make a bad sound.

Tom shows up at 8:00 on Saturday.

Then the dark thing sits up.

His face comes closer and closer.

_____

_____

_____

_____

_____

12. LUIS GETS A JOB

Word Attack

game   You know how **ame** sounds in **game**. Say **c** with **ame**, and you have a new word. Read this word: **came**. Write it in the sentence below.

Carmen _____ home with a big bag.

old   You know the word **old**. See if you can read this word: **told**. Now write the words below. Circle the letter group that is the same in all of them.

told _____   sold _____

cold _____

ea   Remember what works with some words: when you see two vowels together, the first one may sound like its own name. The next one may have no sound at all. Try this with a new word: **mean**. Read the new word **mean**.

Vowels   You can attack the new word **sale**. It ends with **e**, so look at the last three letters. Yes, this is a word that ends with a vowel, another letter, and then **e**. Remember: in many words like this, the **e** has no sound. The other vowel sounds like its own name. Try reading the word: **sale**. Does it work? Yes—the word is **sale**. Write it in this sentence.

The car is not for _____.

Attack another word the same way. Try reading this word: **side**. The letter **i** sounds like its own name, and you can't hear the **e**. Do you know this word? Write it in the sentence.

The door is on the other _____ of the house.

Words to Know

	Look	Say	Picture	Write
around a-round	☐	☐	☐	_____
came	☐	☐	☐	_____

43

	Look	Say	Picture	Write
change	☐	☐	☐	_____
even	☐	☐	☐	_____
far	☐	☐	☐	_____
gone	☐	☐	☐	_____
mean	☐	☐	☐	_____
much	☐	☐	☐	_____
pretty pret-ty	☐	☐	☐	_____
sale	☐	☐	☐	_____
side	☐	☐	☐	_____
told	☐	☐	☐	_____

Word Attack

+s Write **s** after these words to make five new words.

it _____   one _____

own _____   paint _____

sale _____

+'s Write **'s** after **Luis** to get the word **Luis's.** Use this word to show that Luis has something. Write the new word in the sentence.

Did you see _____ ad?

2=1 You can put **him** and **self** together to make a new word: **himself**. Write it in the sentence.

Luis likes to talk about _____.

12. LUIS GETS A JOB

Carmen wants to see Luis's ad again. She goes to the shop. She can't believe what she sees at first. The ad is gone. The wall of the shop looks like new snow—clean! Someone has just been painting it. Carmen goes around to the other side. There, she sees Luis. He is painting.

"What's up, Luis?"

"Carmen!" he says. "I'm so happy to see you. I wanted to tell you how sorry I am about the other day. I did not mean to make a problem for Tom."

"No? Well, you did. That was wrong, Luis."

"I know. I am going to change. No more writing on walls. Just look at me."

"I'm looking. As far as I can see, you're at it again."

"No, no. You don't get it. I'm working for the guy who owns this place. You see, I came back here. I told the guy what I did. I said I want to make it right. I asked what I could do. He gave me this paint. He told me to paint over the graffiti. So here I am."

"Good going, Luis. Maybe you're not a bad guy after all."

But Luis has put down his paint can. He is looking at the wall. "The guy wants it to look new," he says. "But you know what? I think I can make it look even better than new."

Luis takes out another can of paint. Then he takes out another can—and—another—and another. He starts painting a picture on the wall. He paints a pretty beach. He paints little houses. He paints people walking hand in hand.

"Luis!" Carmen lets out a cry. "Don't you get it? This is not what the shop wants. They want the wall to look clean! They did not ask you for this no-good picture."

Just then, the man who owns the shop comes out.

Luis says, "Take a look. You're going to like this. I think it is some of my best work."

"Here we go again," says Carmen to herself.

But then she hears what the man is saying: "This painting is good, Luis. I like it. You really know how to paint."

"Luis is the name. Painting is my game."

"Well, Luis," says the man. "I have a big sale coming up this week. I want someone to paint an ad on my window. Can you do that for me? You can make some money."

"How much?" Luis asks.

"I'll give you $25 for the first one. If I like it, I will ask you to do more. I have sales every other week. So there will be lots of work. Maybe I can give you a little raise after a while. I said maybe. We will have to see. What do you say?"

"It sounds good to me," says Luis. He has a smile on his face. Carmen can see that he feels good about himself. But that is OK with her. She is happy for him.

"I will save up some money," says Luis. "Yes, that's what I'll do. I'll save up some money and get a good, fast bike for myself."

What Do You Think?

Luis does a painting on the wall of the shop. The man likes it. But Luis did not ask if he could do the painting before he started. Was this wrong? Why or why not? Talk about it with a friend or a group of friends.

Putting Ideas in Order

In a story, you do not always hear about things in the order that they happen. Read the sentences below. They tell three things that happen in the story in the order that you read about them. Find the thing that happens first in time. Write that sentence on the line.

Luis paints over the walls of the shop.

Luis tells the man at the shop that he did the graffiti.

Luis is asked to paint an ad for the shop.

_____

_____

_____

Describe It

When the man comes out of the shop, he sees a painting on the wall. The words below tell three details seen in the painting. One or more words in the story describe each detail. Write these words on the lines. Look back at the story if you have to.

The painting shows a _____ beach, _____

houses, and people _____.

What is the painting like? All three people in this story describe it. Here are some of the words they say.

        my best work   no-good   good

Who says what? Write the group of words next to the names below.

Luis: _____

Carmen: _____

The man who owns the shop: _____

13. LUIS AND THE BIG BIKE SALE

Luis wants a bike. But he wants to save money, too. Then he sees an ad for a bike sale. *Just what I need,* he thinks. He gets to the sale as fast as he can. But there is already a long line at the shop.

Luis takes his place at the end of the line. He waits. The line does not move much. *The best bikes will be gone,* he thinks.

Then he has an idea. He will make up a story to pass the time in line. He says to himself, "What am I doing here? I should be at that other sale." He makes up a name, **Fire Mountain Bikes**. "Yes. That's it. **Fire Mountain Bikes.** They have a better sale than the one at this shop. You can get a bike for $100 there. The same bike is going for $200 here. Where is this **Fire Mountain Bikes**? Luis makes up a place far, far away. It's a long drive from here. But you can save $100 on a bike."

Really? Luis thinks. *That's worth a drive. He will not tell the other people in line or they will start talking about the sale at* **Fire Mountain Bikes.** *But one man knows about the sale at* **Fire Mountain Bikes.** *He is telling all the people in the line. When people start talking about the sale, everyone will go there.*

"Where is this **Fire Mountain Bikes**?" a girl asks.

"What's that about another sale?" a man asks.

"It's a long drive from here. But you can save $100 on a bike," says the girl.

"Really?" says the man. "That's worth a drive." Many people start talking about the sale at **Fire Mountain Bikes.**

Why am I even here? thinks Luis. *I should be at that other sale.*

But a lot more is going through his mind by this time. All this talk about another sale is getting to him. *What if there really is another sale?* he thinks. *What if there is a* **Fire Mountain Bikes**? *Everyone else believes it. Could so many people be wrong? I don't think so. They say I can get a bike there for $100. So why am I waiting to buy that same bike here for $200? I will be one sorry man if I do that. I had better get over to the other sale right away.*

Just then the line starts to move. Luis laughs to himself as he thinks, "Boy! I started to believe my own made-up story. I'll just stay in line and buy my bike." That is just what Luis did.

Putting Ideas in Order

Read the sentences below. They tell five things that happen in the story. Write them in the order that they happen.

People start talking about the other sale.

Luis thinks he will go to the other sale.

The line does not move much.

Luis makes up a story about another sale.

Luis sees an ad for a bike sale.

_____

_____

_____

_____

_____

_____

_____

_____

Remembering Details

Write a word from the story on each line. Look back at the story if you have to.

Luis goes to a shop to buy a _____.

When he gets there, he finds a _____.

Luis makes up a story about a better _____.

He makes up a shop that he calls _____

_____ Bikes.

50

14. THE BASEBALL PLAYER, 1

Word Attack

game You know the word **game**. It sounds like the new word **fame**. Try reading this word: **fame**. Write the three words below on the lines. Circle the letter group that is in all of them.

fame _____   game _____

same _____

not The letters **ot** are in **not** and **lot**. Find the same letters in **got**. Try reading this word: **got**. Write the new word in the sentence below.

I _____ some money at the bank.

find You can attack the word **behind**. Just take it apart. See it as two letter groups: **be** and **hind**. You know the word **be**. And you can read **hind**. You know how the word **find** sounds. It sounds the same way here. Just take away the **f**. Say **h** with **ind**. Now try reading the word: **behind**. Then write the words below. Circle the letters that are the same in all of them.

behind _____   mind _____

find _____

Take a Guess

The word **through** does not sound the way it looks. But you know how the first three letters sound. You have seen them in **throw**. Now read the sentence below. See if you can guess the word in dark letters from the other words around it.

Look **through** the window.

Did you guess the word? Write it here. _____

51

Words to Know

	Look	Say	Picture	Write
behind be-hind	☐	☐	☐	_____
done	☐	☐	☐	_____
fame	☐	☐	☐	_____
got	☐	☐	☐	_____
now	☐	☐	☐	_____
their	☐	☐	☐	_____
through	☐	☐	☐	_____
till	☐	☐	☐	_____
turn	☐	☐	☐	_____

Word Attack

+s Write these words with an **s** ending. Make seven new words.

base _____   change _____

player _____   write _____

work _____   new _____

turn _____

+ing Write the words below with the ending **ing**:

play _____   show _____

2=1 You know the words below. Put them together to make two new words. Write the new words on the line.

on + to = _____   your + self = _____

14. THE BASEBALL PLAYER, 1

Part 1

This two-part play happens in two places. **Part 1** takes place outside, close to Tom and Carmen's school. Carmen is with Tom when the play starts. The school can be seen behind the two friends.

Carmen: Did you hear the news, Tom? Luis got a job. He works for that fish shop now. They like the way he paints. They want him to paint an ad on their window. If he does OK, I guess they will ask him to do more.

Tom: Too much! **(He lets out a laugh.)** You mean Luis gets money to do graffiti now?

Carmen: That's one way to look at it. I don't know. Luis says he's going through a lot of changes. Maybe he's going to stop showing off so much.

Tom: I'll believe that when I see it!

(Luis comes in. He has some food in one hand. He gives Carmen a wave. Then he turns to Tom.)

Luis: Say, I hear you play baseball, Tom. How are things going with that?

Tom: **(with a cold look)** Not too bad.

Luis: Do you need some players? I'm not with a team right now.

Tom: Oh, you play baseball, too, do you?

Luis: Are you kidding? Playing baseball is what I do best. They don't call me **Hot Dog** for nothing. I have done some things that even I can't believe. You should see me going around the bases. One time, I hit this home run—well. There is no use going into it. I will be in the Hall of Fame someday. That's all I can say.

Carmen: Same old Luis.

Luis: How about it, Tom? Can I play on your team?

Tom: You ask for a lot, Luis. Maybe I can take you in to meet the coach. But that's all. I want to see you play first.

53

Luis: No problem. There is a field behind my house. Let's go play right now. You can see for yourself how good I am.

Tom: But we need one more player. We need someone to field.

Luis: **(looks at Carmen)** How about you? Don't you play a little?

Carmen: A little.

Luis: Well, then! Let's go.

What Do You Think?

Put yourself in Tom's place. Would you help Luis? Why or why not? Meet with one or more friends who have read **Part 1** of this play. Talk about what Tom should do. Did you ever help someone who had done a bad thing to you? Were you happy that you helped, or were you sorry? Why?

Remembering Details

The sentences below ask about details in the play so far. Write the answers on the lines. Look back at the play as much as you need to.

The kids are outside in this part of the play. What are they close to? _____

Luis says he plays baseball so well that people have a name for him. What is the name? _____

Who will play with Tom and Luis? _____

Where will they play? _____

What Will Happen Next?

All the sentences below tell things that **may** happen next. What do you think **will** happen? Write your idea on the line. Talk about it with a friend who has read **The Baseball Player, 1.** Tell your friend why you think this will happen. See what your friend thinks.

Tom will find that Luis plays better than he does.

Luis will talk big but will not play well.

Luis will get mad and not play at all.

_____
_____
_____
_____

McR

15. THE BASEBALL PLAYER, 2

Part 2

This part of the play takes place in a field behind Luis's house. Carmen, Tom, and Luis are playing baseball. Tom throws the ball to Luis. Luis throws it to Carmen. You do not need a real baseball for this. The players can just make the moves.

Tom: Let's try playing for real. We can take turns hitting. Luis, you're up first.

Luis: (tries to hit the ball but can't) Oh! So close!

Tom: Close is nothing. You didn't get a hit.

Carmen: Next time, Luis.

Tom: Your turn, Carmen. I'll throw, you hit. Luis, let's see how you field.

Carmen: (hits the ball) All right!

Luis (runs back) I have it! I have it! I have it! Oh! **(He stops and looks back.)** I had it.

(A big man comes in from the right. Tom looks up and sees him.)

Tom: Coach! What are you doing here?

Coach: I was just taking a walk. I saw you kids playing. Tom, I think you have a real player here.

Luis: That was nothing. I'm a little sick today. You should see me at my best.

Coach: I didn't mean you, guy. I'm talking about this girl. **(He looks at Carmen.)** How would you like to be part of our team?

Carmen: I hardly know what to say. How many girls will be on the team?

Coach: With you, you mean?

Carmen: Yes.

Coach: One.

Carmen: I'll have to think about it, Coach.

What Do You Think?

Put yourself in Carmen's place. Would you take a place on the team if you were the only girl? Meet with a friend or in a small group. Talk about what you think Carmen should do. Give your reasons why.

Remembering Details

The sentences below ask about details in the play. Write the answers. An answer can be one word, a group of words, or a sentence. Look back at the play if you need to.

Who is playing? _____

Who gets the first hit? _____

Who throws the ball? _____

What does Luis do after he tries to hit? _____

Finding the One Big Idea

The sentence below should tell the big idea of the play. Only one of the three groups of words will end the sentence in this way. Find that group of words. Write it on the line.

After Coach sees the kids playing baseball, _____
_____
_____

a. Luis lets him know he feels a little sick.

b. he asks Carmen—not Luis—to play for the team.

c. he tells Tom he is taking a little walk.

16. A CARD FOR CARMEN

Word Attack

smile You know the word **smile**. Change the first two letters to **wh**, and you have one of your new words. Try reading this word: **while**. (Remember that **w** and **h** together make one sound.) Write the two words below. Circle the letters that are the same.

while _____   smile _____

just You know the word **just**. The letter group **ust** always sounds the same. Try reading this word: **must**. Write the words below. Circle the letter groups that are the same in them.

just _____   must _____

hard You know the word **hard**. The word **card** ends with the same letter group. The **c** in **card** has a **k** sound. Try reading the word **card**. Do you know this word? Write it in the sentence. Then circle the letter group **ard** in it.

Tom wants to buy a _____ for his mom.

look You have seen the letter group **ook** in **look**. It has the same sound in **took**. Read this word: **took**. Write the words below. Circle the letter group that is the same in them.

took _____   look _____

mad You know the word **mad.** If you put **s** in place of **m** you get one of the new **Words to Know**. Try reading the word: **sad**. Write the words you see below. Circle the letter group they all have.

sad _____ mad _____ bad _____ had _____

safe The word **safe** ends with a vowel, another letter, and **e**. In this word, the **e** has no sound. The **a** sounds like the letter **a**. Try to read the new word: **safe**. Write it in the sentence below.

She runs into the house. There she feels _____.

58

Words to Know

	Look	Say	Picture	Write
been	☐	☐	☐	_____
before be-fore	☐	☐	☐	_____
card	☐	☐	☐	_____
must	☐	☐	☐	_____
room	☐	☐	☐	_____
sad	☐	☐	☐	_____
safe	☐	☐	☐	_____
took	☐	☐	☐	_____
under un-der	☐	☐	☐	_____
while	☐	☐	☐	_____

Word Attack

+s   Write an **s** after each word below.

card _____   meet _____

+ed   Write **happen** with **ed** at the end of the word.

_____

+'s   You know the word **dog**. Write **'s** after **dog.**

_____

Now write this new word in the sentence below.

A _____ mouth is not really clean.

2=1   You know the words below. Put them together to make four new words. Write the new words.

in + side = _____

out + side = _____

who + ever = _____

any + one = _____

16. A CARD FOR CARMEN

Many cards and letters have come to the house. Inez looks through them. She sees something for Carmen. But Carmen is not home. The outside of the letter does not say who it is from. Inez wants to open it. She knows this would be wrong, so she holds off. But after a while, she gets sick of waiting for Carmen. She just has to see who the letter is from. She opens it.

Inside, she finds a pretty card. She opens that. "I'm not going to read it," she says to herself. But she does. She does not read much. But she can tell a lot from just the words. She can tell the card is from a boy. She can tell he likes Carmen. She does not have time to see his name. But she thinks, *It must be from Tom. What other guy would write like that to Carmen?*

Now, Inez feels a little scared. Carmen will see that she has looked at her card. She will be mad about it. Inez puts the card behind a painting. Then she puts it under a box. Then she takes it out. *I have done wrong*, she thinks. *I have to face up to it.* She leaves the card where Carmen will see it.

Inez sits in her room for a long time. Carmen does not come home. At last, Inez comes out. The house is dark. She turns on some lights. The card is gone. Right away, Inez knows what has happened. The dog took it. A cold feeling goes through her. *I should have put it somewhere safe*, she thinks. She looks all over. At last, she finds the card. Yes, she was right. This card has been in a dog's mouth. It has gone through a sad change. It is no longer clean. It is not what anyone would call pretty. A dog's mouth can do that to a card. Many of the words are hard to read. Some of them are gone.

Inez does not see Tom's name. That part is inside the dog. She reads the other part. The boy writes that he wants Carmen to come over. He writes that he has something to tell her.

It must be from Tom, Inez thinks. *What other guy would ask Carmen to come over?* Inez has not been to Tom's house before. But the card tells where the house is.

I will go over there, she thinks. *I will go right now. I will tell him what happened and say I'm sorry. Everything will be all right.*

At the door, Inez stops. *I may as well wear something pretty*, she thinks.

She goes back to her room to change.

You Make the Call

Inez opens a letter that is for someone else. Put yourself in Inez's place. The letter is now open. You did it. You know it was wrong. But what's done is done. What should you do now? Hide the letter? Tell Carmen what you did? Talk to the writer? Get together with a group of three or four friends, and talk about the story. Talk about the bigger idea, too. If you do something wrong, what should you do next? As you talk, write down some of the ideas your group comes up with.

Describe It

The groups of words below are from the story. They all describe the card. But some of them describe how the card looks at first. Some describe how it looks that night. Think where the words should go. Write them on the lines.

sad   words are gone   pretty   clean

How the card looks at first	How the card looks that night
_____	_____
_____	_____
_____	_____
_____	_____

Put Ideas in Order

The sentences below tell four things that happen in the story. Write them in the order that they happen.

The card has gone through a sad change.

Inez opens Carmen's letter.

The card is gone.

Inez tries to hide the card behind a painting.

_____
_____
_____
_____
_____

17. INEZ MEETS A BOY

Inez has come to a big apartment house. There are old cars around the place. One car has a smashed up window. There is lots of graffiti on the side of the house. It looks pretty bad here. It does not look like much of a home.

Inez looks at the card and then at the house.

Well, this must be the place, she thinks. *I guess Tom's family doesn't have much money.*

The door is open. Inez goes through it. Inside she finds a long hall. There is only one light in the hall. It is at the other end, far away. So the hall is pretty dark. Inez walks along till she finds the apartment she is looking for. *Should I ring?*, she thinks. Then she thinks, *Why not? I have come this far. I will ring.*

A boy opens the door. He looks a little like Tom. But he is not Tom.

"Yes?" the boy says.

"Is Tom home?" she asks.

"I don't know," says the boy. "Why don't you go to his house and find out? This is my house. Who are you?"

"I'm Inez. I'm Carmen's sister."

"Oh." The boy looks down. He sees the card in Inez's hand. "Well, Carmen's sister or whoever you are, what are you doing with my card?"

"Your card?" Inez throws him a look. "This is from Tom." Then she stops. She sees that she may be wrong. "Isn't it?"

"I know my own writing when I see it," says the boy.

Now Inez feels lost. "Just who are you?" she asks.

"My name is Luis."

"Luis! You mean—**The** Luis?"

"The one and only." Luis is wearing a big smile now.

"The boy who makes people laugh?" says Inez.

A change comes over Luis's face. He looks sad. "Yes. I guess that's me," he says. Then he asks Inez, "Do you like the painting on that card?"

"It's really pretty," says Inez. "Or should I say—it was."

His face lights up again. "I did that," says Luis. "That is what I wanted to tell Carmen. I have a new way to make money now. A card shop wants to buy my paintings. They are going to use them to make cards."

"Really? Boy, that's something. You must be a pretty good painter."

"Yes." Luis likes the way Inez is looking at him. "I am pretty good. Maybe the best that you will ever see. Would you like to see some of my paintings some time?"

"How about right now?" says Inez.

"Well!" says Luis. "I like the way you talk, Carmen's sister. Come on in."

Describe It

The words below name things you would see around Luis' home. Find words in the story that describe these things. Write one word on every line.

_____ apartment house

_____ cars

_____ car window

_____ hall

_____ light

Remembering Details

The sentences below ask about the story. Write the answers on the line. You may write one word or more than one on a line. Look back at the story if you need to.

What is on the side of Luis' house? _____

Where is the light in the hall? _____

What does Luis see in Inez's hand? _____

What does Inez say about the painting on the card? _____

Who is now going to buy paintings from Luis? _____

Find the One Big Idea

These sentences tell about the story. One sentence tells what the story is all about. Find that sentence. Write it on the lines below.

Inez does not get to see Tom after all.

Inez meets Luis and likes him.

Luis finds out that Inez is Carmen's sister.

_____

_____

_____

MEMORY CHIPS

Remember to keep working with your memory chips. They will help you remember these words. Keep your memory chips in two groups. One group you are working with every day. The other group about once a week. Go over them just to make sure. Keep up the good work. You have come a long way.

We two are **alike**.	IA	**Read** the word.	IA	The **word** is out.	IA
Take Mack **along**.	IA	I'm **reading** a story.	IA	The story has many **words**.	IA
It comes **apart.**	IA	He **reads** the ad.	IA	**Write** me a letter.	IA
The dog will **attack**.	IA	I feel the **same** way.	IA	He is the **writer** of the story.	IA
Look out **below**!	IA	Say the **sentence**.	IA	He is **writing** it now.	IA
Circle the word.	IA	Write two **sentences**.	IA	I'm **as** mad **as** you are.	1A
Group them together.	IA	How does it **sound**?	IA	Put it in the **box**.	1A
I have two **groups** of friends.	IA	I hear the **sounds** of the sea.	IA	Here are two **boxes.**	1A
The **introduction** comes first.	IA	Tell us a **story**.	IA	Put me **down**.	1A
Write a **letter**.	IA	Put **these** away.	IA	**Tom's** car goes fast.	1A
This word has three **letters**.	IA	We can go **together**.	IA	Tom **has** a car.	1A

word	IB	read	IB	alike	IB
words	IB	reading	IB	along	IB
write	IB	reads	IB	apart	IB
writer	IB	same	IB	attack	IB
writing	IB	sentence	IB	below	IB
as	IB	sentences	IB	circle	IB
box	IB	sound	IB	group	IB
boxes	IB	sounds	IB	groups	IB
down	IB	story	IB	introduction	IB
Tom's	1B	these	IB	letter	IB
has	1B	together	IB	letters	IB

The car is **here**.	1A	She **sits** by Mom.	1A	**Everything** is OK now.	3A
He can **leave** it here.	1A	I hear **someone**.	1A	I have looked **everywhere**.	3A
He **leaves** the car there.	1A	Buy **something** for me.	1A	Have you **had** dinner?	3A
Robin is her **name**.	1A	What is that **thing**?	1A	My name is **Inez**.	3A
I have **nothing** to hide.	1A	Take your **things** and go.	1A	That is **Inez's** sister.	3A
Grandma is **old**.	1A	We cook in the **kitchen**.	3A	She **isn't** my sister.	3A
I **open** the window.	1A	Tom **made** dinner.	3A	Don't give her **anything**.	3A
She **opens** the door.	1A	Who plays **better**?	3A	It's the **last** day of school.	3A
Is it here **or** there?	1A	They **called** him Jake.	3A	**Let** me out.	3A
Do what is **right**.	1A	**Carmen** is a girl.	3A	She **lets** him go.	3A
Come **sit** down.	1A	Look in **every** room.	3A	He will **show** it to you.	3A

everything	3B	sits	1B	here	1B
everywhere	3B	someone	1B	leave	1B
had	3B	something	1B	leaves	1B
Inez	3B	thing	1B	name	1B
Inez's	3B	things	1B	nothing	1B
isn't	3B	kitchen	3B	old	1B
kitchen	3B	made	3B	open	1B
last	3B	better	3B	opens	1B
let	3B	called	3B	or	1B
lets	3B	Carmen	3B	right	1B
show	3B	every	3B	sit	1B

The girls are **sisters**.	3A	Tell me the **details**.	5A	Do you **remember** that day?	5A
They are **so** alike.	3A	Give **each** boy a job.	5A	**Remembering** can be hard.	5A
I want to go, **too**.	3A	Stop at the **end**.	5A	The letter **e** is a **vowel**	5A
She paints **pictures**.	5A	The game is **ending**.	5A	I like that **guy**.	6A
Play it **again**.	5A	I like happy **endings**.	5A	I like you **anyway**.	6A
The food is **all** gone.	5A	Tie the 2 **ends** of string together.	5A	**He's** a good guy.	6A
Answer me.	5A	**Guess** my name.	5A	She **believes** his story.	6A
She knows the **answers**.	5A	Put the words in **order**.	5A	Luis **cries** when he is hit.	6A
Mom likes her **best**.	5A	Stop **ordering** me around.	5A	**Everyone** likes Carmen.	6A
Describe Tom to her.	5A	I have a **picture** of you.	5A	I have won—**face** it.	6A
Tell me every **detail**.	5A	All words have **vowels**.	5A	They come **from** me.	6A

remember	5B	details	5B	sisters	3B
remembering	5B	each	5B	so	3B
vowel	5B	end	5B	too	3B
guy	6B	ending	5B	pictures	5B
anyway	6B	endings	5B	again	5B
he's	6B	ends	5B	all	5B
believes	6B	guess	5B	answer	5B
cries	6B	order	5B	answers	5B
everyone	6B	ordering	5B	best	5B
face	6B	picture	5B	describe	5B
from	6B	vowels	5B	detail	5B

The girls **were** laughing. 6A	Luis **tries** hard. 6A	I see **lights**. 8A
He **asked** if she were ill. 6A	I don't feel **well**. 6A	**Luis** is a boy. 8A
I **would** like to know. 6A	Is it **wrong** to laugh? 6A	**Move** fast. 8A
Let's go home. 6A	**Why** do you laugh? 6A	Where are we **now**? 8A
Keep me in **mind**. 6A	She **moves** the car. 6A	This **place** is our home 8A
Tom **said** something bad. 6A	He looks at **himself.** 8A	I have seen many **places**. 8A
Donna **saw** him today. 6A	You **always** say that. 8A	**Point** out your sister. 8A
Somehow it will get done. 6A	Say something **else**. 8A	She **points** to Inez. 8A
You are bigger **than** I. 6A	A dog has **feelings** too. 8A	She points to her own **self**. 8A
That's my house. 6A	Get that one **first** 8A	Kay **shops** for food. 8A
There is no school **today**. 6A	Kids play **games**. 8A	Inez **shows** up. 8A

lights	8B	tries	6B	were	6B
Luis	8B	well	6B	asked	6B
move	8B	wrong	6B	would	6B
now	8B	why	6B	let's	6B
place	8B	moves	8B	mind	6B
places	8B	himself	8B	said	6B
point	8B	always	8B	saw	6B
points	8B	else	8B	somehow	6B
self	8B	feelings	8B	than	6B
shops	8B	first	8B	that's	6B
shows	8B	games	8B	today	6B

Let's go out **someday**. 8A	**She's** at home. 10A	She's on your **side**. 12A
Talk to **them**. 8A	What will **happen**? 10A	Have you **told** her? 12A
Yes, I will. 8A	It **happens** too fast. 10A	It's **around** here. 12A
They meet **again**. 10A	Kay goes home by **herself**. 10A	Luis **came** home. 12A
Buy me a car, Dad. 10A	Do your **homework**. 10A	Don't **change** your mind. 12A
Carmen's mom is home. 10A	Put the food in your **mouth**. 10A	**Even** Dad likes it. 12A
I **could** buy 2 cars. 10A	The car **moves** too fast. 10A	School is **far** away. 12A
Open the **door**. 10A	**Oh**, what a day! 10A	The money is **gone**. 12A
It's **somewhere** close by. 10A	**Pull** the door open. 10A	He laughs at **himself**. 12A
This is dog **food**. 10A	She **pulls** Tom's hand. 10A	Every dog has **its** day. 12A
Hand me the ball. 10A	I will **save** some money. 10A	That is **Luis's** bike. 12A

side	12B	she's	10B	someday	8B
told	12B	happen	10B	them	8B
around	12B	happens	10B	yes	8B
came	12B	herself	10B	again	10B
change	12B	homework	10B	buy	10B
even	12B	mouth	10B	Carmen's	10B
far	12B	moves	10B	could	10B
gone	12B	oh	10B	door	10B
himself	12B	pull	10B	somewhere	10B
its	12B	pulls	10B	food	10B
Luis's	12B	save	10B	hand	10B

Say what you **mean**. 12A	Get **yourself** a drink. 14A	Go **through** the hall. 14A
There isn't **much** time. 12A	He **writes** a letter. 14A	It **happened** before. 16A
Who **owns** this shop? 12A	I want **fame** and money. 14A	A boy **meets** a girl. 16A
Jake **paints** houses. 12A	Donna **got** sick. 14A	You **must** not cry. 16A
What a **pretty** picture! 12A	Here is the good **news**. 14A	Go to your **room**. 16A
My dog is not for **sale**. 12A	Dad **works** hard. 14A	I don't feel **safe**. 16A
I go to lots of **sales**. 12A	They do **their** work. 14A	He told a **sad** story. 16A
She **changes** her mind. 14A	These **players** are good. 14A	He's **been** to the bank. 16A
What have you **done**? 14A	The bus will **turn** around. 14A	Get home **before** dark. 16A
Run around the **bases**. 14A	They are **showing** off. 14A	Do you know this **card** game? 16A
Our team is **behind**. 14A	It's **under** the picture. 16A	He **took** my money. 16A

through	14B	yourself	14B	mean	12B
happened	16B	writes	14B	much	12B
meets	16B	fame	14B	owns	12B
must	16B	got	14B	paints	12B
room	16B	news	14B	pretty	12B
safe	16B	works	14B	sale	12B
sad	16B	their	14B	sales	12B
been	16B	players	14B	changes	14B
before	16B	turn	14B	done	14B
card	16B	showing	14B	bases	14B
took	16B	under	16B	behind	14B

| Go away **while** I read. 16A | I'll write my **cards** myself. 16A | It is cold **outside**. 16A |
| The dog is **inside** the house. 16A | Come in **whoever** you are. 16A | That is the **dog's** house. 16A |

| outside | 16B | cards | 16B | while | 16B |
| dog's | 16B | whoever | 16B | inside | 16B |